HOMER

GREE
FC

BY

WILLIAM BISHOP OWEN, Ph.D.

AND

EDGAR JOHNSON GOODSPEED, Ph.D.

THE UNIVERSITY OF CHICAGO

CHICAGO
THE UNIVERSITY OF CHICAGO PRESS
1909

708678

COPYRIGHT 1906 BY
THE UNIVERSITY OF CHICAGO

Published November 1906
Second edition August 1909

C

Composed and Printed By
The University of Chicago Press
Chicago, Illinois, U. S. A.

This series of word-lists is the outgrowth of the conviction that the ordinary way of acquiring Homeric vocabulary is both wasteful and ineffectual. The chief difficulty in learning to read Homer lies in the large and varied character of the vocabulary required, and these lists have been prepared in order to help the student to learn Homeric words in a systematic and practical way. A moderate number of words learned each day and constantly reviewed will rapidly enlarge the student's working vocabulary, and steadily better his equipment for sight-reading. He will gradually be emancipated from the constant use of the lexicon, while his knowledge of Greek words will gain rather than lose in precision and permanence. Each day a few new words should be learned, and those previously learned should be rapidly reviewed. The student will very shortly find himself possessed of a vocabulary which will greatly facilitate the work of translation, and make the reading of Homer at sight a pleasant and natural exercise. In short, it is believed that the mastery of these lists will secure for the student that much-talked-of thing, the ability to read Homer; and make of his study of it a means, not simply of discipline, but of enjoyment and culture.

THE EDITORS

THE UNIVERSITY OF CHICAGO

PREFACE TO THE SECOND EDITION

The demand for a new edition of these lists has given us the opportunity to correct some misprints and to modify a few definitions. The numberings remain unchanged throughout. Attention may be called to the fact that in the statistics of verb occurrences, compounds have been reckoned with their primitives. In this we have followed the procedure of Gehring's *Index Homericus*, upon the materials of which our statistics are based.

THE EDITORS

THE UNIVERSITY OF CHICAGO
, August 1, 1909

CONTENTS

GREEK LISTS

VERBS

I. Verbs occurring 500–2,000 times	3
II. Verbs occurring 200–500 times	3
III. Verbs occurring 100–200 times	3
IV. Verbs occurring 50–100 times	4
V. Verbs occurring 25–50 times	5
VI. Verbs occurring 10–25 times	6

NOUNS

VII. Nouns occurring 500–1,000 times	11
VIII. Nouns occurring 200–500 times	11
IX. Nouns occurring 100–200 times	11
X. Nouns occurring 50–100 times	12
XI. Nouns occurring 25–50 times	13
XII. Nouns occurring 10–25 times	14

PRONOUNS, ADJECTIVES, ADVERBS, PREPOSITIONS, ETC.

XIII. Pronouns, adjectives, adverbs, prepositions, etc., occurring 500–10,000 times	21
XIV. Pronouns, adjectives, adverbs, prepositions, etc., occurring 200–500 times	21
XV. Pronouns, adjectives, adverbs, prepositions, etc., occurring 100–200 times	22
XVI. Pronouns, adjectives, adverbs, prepositions, etc., occurring 50–100 times	22
XVII. Pronouns, adjectives, adverbs, prepositions, etc., occurring 25–50 times	23
XVIII. Pronouns, adjectives, adverbs, prepositions, etc., occurring 10–25 times	25

CONTENTS

ENGLISH LISTS

VERBS

I. Verbs occurring 500–2,000 times 33
II. Verbs occurring 200–500 times 33
III. Verbs occurring 100–200 times 33
IV. Verbs occurring 50–100 times 34
V. Verbs occurring 25–50 times 35
VI. Verbs occurring 10–25 times 37

NOUNS

VII. Nouns occurring 500–1,000 times 43
VIII. Nouns occurring 200–500 times 43
IX. Nouns occurring 100–200 times 43
X. Nouns occurring 50–100 times 44
XI. Nouns occurring 25–50 times 45
XII. Nouns occurring 10–25 times 46

PRONOUNS, ADJECTIVES, ADVERBS, PREPOSITIONS, ETC.

XIII. Pronouns, adjectives, adverbs, prepositions, etc., occurring 500–10,000 times 53
XIV. Pronouns, adjectives, adverbs, prepositions, etc., occurring 200–500 times 53
XV. Pronouns, adjectives, adverbs, prepositions, etc., occurring 100–200 times 54
XVI. Pronouns, adjectives, adverbs, prepositions, etc., occurring 50–100 times 55
XVII. Pronouns, adjectives, adverbs, prepositions, etc., occurring 25–50 times 56
XVIII. Pronouns, adjectives, adverbs, prepositions, etc., occurring 10–25 times 58

GREEK LISTS

VERBS

LIST I
VERBS OCCURRING 500–2,000 TIMES

1 ἄγω
2 βαίνω
3 βάλλω
4 δίδωμι
5 εἰμί
6 εἶμι
7 εἶπον
8 ἔρχομαι
9 ἔχω
10 ἵστημι
11 ὁράω
12 τίθημι
13 φημί

LIST II
VERBS OCCURRING 200–500 TIMES

14 αἱρέω
15 ἀμείβω
16 αὐδάω
17 γίγνομαι
18 ἐθέλω
19 ἕπω
20 ἵημι
21 ἱκνέομαι
22 κεῖμαι
23 κτείνω
24 λείπω
25 μένω
26 οἶδα
27 ὄλλυμι
28 ὄρνυμι
29 πείθω
30 πίπτω
31 φέρω
32 φεύγω
33 φωνέω
34 χέω

LIST III
VERBS OCCURRING 100–200 TIMES

35 ἀγορεύω
36 ἀΐσσω
37 ἀκούω
38 ἀμύνω
39 ἀνώγω
40 ἄρχω
41 γιγνώσκω
42 δάμνημι
43 δείδω
44 δέχομαι
45 δύναμαι
46 δύω
47 ἐάω
48 ἕζομαι
49 εἴρω
50 ἐλάω
51 ἔοικα
52 ἐρύω
53 εὔχομαι
54 ἧμαι
55 θνῄσκω
56 ἱκάνω
57 καλέω
58 καλύπτω
59 κελεύω
60 κίω
61 κλύω
62 λαμβάνω
63 λέγω
64 λύω

HOMERIC VOCABULARIES

65 μάχομαι
66 μέμαα
67 μιμνήσκω
68 ναίω
69 νέομαι
70 νοέω
71 οἴχομαι
72 ὀίω
73 ὀτρύνω

74 πάσχω
75 παύω
76 πέλω
77 πέμπω
78 πνείω
79 ῥέζω
80 σεύω
81 τελέω
82 τέρπω

83 τεύχω
84 τίπτω
85 τρέπω
86 φαίνω, φάω
87 φράζομαι
88 φρονέω
89 χαίρω

LIST IV

VERBS OCCURRING 50-100 TIMES

90 ἀγείρω
91 ἅλλομαι
92 ἀνάσσω
93 ἅπτω
94 ἀραρίσκω
95 ἄχνυμαι
96 δαίνυμι
97 δέω
98 ἐγείρω
99 ἕδω
100 εἴδομαι
101 εἴρομαι
102 ἕλκω
103 ἔλπω
104 ἕννυμι
105 ἔρδω
106 ἐρύκω
107 εὕδω
108 εὑρίσκω
109 ζώω
110 ἠμί

111 θέω
112 ἵζω
113 ἴσχω
114 καίω
115 κέλομαι
116 κιχάνω
117 κλαίω
118 κλίνω
119 κρίνω
120 λανθάνω
121 λίσσομαι
122 μάρναμαι
123 μαχέομαι
124 μέλλω
125 μέλω
126 μίμνω
127 μίσγω, μίγνυμι
128 μυθέομαι
129 νέμω
130 νοστέω
131 ὀδύρομαι

132 ὀνομάζω
133 ὀπάζω
134 ὁρμάω
135 ὀρούω
136 πειράω
137 πέρθω
138 πέτομαι
139 πίμπλημι
140 πίνω
141 πλήσσω
142 ποιέω
143 πολεμίζω
144 πόρον
145 πυνθάνομαι
146 ῥέω
147 ῥήγνυμι
148 σαόω
149 στρέφω
150 τάμνω
151 τανύω
152 ἐπιτέλλω

VERBS OCCURRING 25–50 TIMES

153 τίω
154 τλάω
155 τρέφω
156 ἔπεφνον
157 φθίνω
158 φιλέω
159 φορέω
160 χολόω
161 ὠθέω

LIST V
VERBS OCCURRING 25–50 TIMES

162 ἀγγέλλω
163 ἄγνυμι
164 ἀγοράομαι
165 ἀείδω
166 αἰδέομαι
167 αἰνέω
168 ἀκαχίζω
169 ἀκοντίζω
170 ἀλάομαι
171 ἀλεείνω
172 ἀλέξω
173 ἀλεύομαι
174 ἀλύσκω
175 ἁμαρτάνω
176 ἀνδάνω
177 ἀπαυράω
178 ἀπειλέω
179 ἀπιθέω
180 ἀποαίνυμαι
181 ἀράομαι
182 ἄρνυμαι
183 ἁρπάζω
184 αὔω
185 βοάω
186 βουλεύω
187 βούλομαι
188 γαμέω
189 γείνομαι
190 γελόω
191 γηθέω
192 γοάω
193 δαήσεαι
194 δαίω
195 δατέομαι
196 δείκνυμι
197 δεύομαι
198 διώκω
199 δοκέω
200 δουπέω
201 δύνω
202 ἐέργω, ἔργομαι
203 εἴκω
204 εἴλω
205 ἐλαύνω
206 ἐλεαίρω
207 ἐλεέω
208 ἐναρίζω
209 ἐνέπω
210 ἐπείγω
211 ἐπίσταμαι
212 ἐρεείνω
213 ἐρείδω
214 ἐρείπω
215 ἐρέω
216 ἐρίζω
217 ἐσθίω
218 ἡγεμονεύω
219 ἡγέομαι
220 θαυμάζω
221 θρώσκω
222 θωρήσσω
223 ἰάλλω
224 ἰάχω
225 ἱερεύω
226 ἰθύνω
227 ἴκω
228 κάμνω
229 κείρω
230 κεύθω
231 κήδω
232 κοιμάω
233 κομίζω
234 κόπτω
235 κορύσσω
236 κυλίνδω
237 λαγχάνω
238 λάμπω
239 λήγω
240 λήθω
241 λούω
242 μενεαίνω

HOMERIC VOCABULARIES

243 μερμηρίζω
244 μεταλλάω
245 μήδομαι
246 μνάομαι
247 μογέω
248 ναιετάω
249 νεικέω
250 νεμεσάω
251 νεύω
252 νικάω
253 νύσσω
254 νωμάω
255 ὀλοφύρομαι
256 ὄμνυμι
257 ὁπλίζω
258 ὀρέγνυμι

259 ὀρίνω
260 ὁρμαίνω
261 οὐτάζω
262 οὐτάω
263 ὀφείλω
264 ὀχθέω
265 παπταίνω
266 πελάζω
267 περάω
268 πήγνυμι
269 πλάζω
270 πλέω
271 πονέομαι
272 πρήσσω
273 σπένδω
274 στενάχω

275 τείνω
276 τείρω
277 τελευτάω
278 τιμάω
279 τίνω
280 τρέχω
281 τυγχάνω
282 τύπτω
283 φθάνω
284 φοβέω
285 φυλάσσω
286 φύω
287 χάζομαι
288 χαρίζω
289 χώομαι
290 χωρέω

LIST VI

VERBS OCCURRING 10–25 TIMES

291 ἀάω
292 ἄγαμαι
293 ἀέξω
294 ἄημι
295 αἴδομαι
296 αἰσχύνω
297 αἰτέω
298 αἰτίζω
299 ἀίω
300 ἀκέομαι
301 ἀλαπάζω
302 ἀλέγω
303 ἀλείφω

304 ἁλίσκομαι
305 ἀμάω
306 ἀναίνομαι
307 ἀντάω
308 ἀντιάω
309 ἀντιβολέω
310 ἀντιόω
311 ἄντομαι
312 ἀνύω
313 ἀπατάω
314 ἀραβέω
315 ἀράσσω
316 ἀρέσκω

317 ἀρήγω
318 ἀριστεύω
319 ἀρκέω
320 ἀρνέομαι
321 ἀρτύνω
322 ἀσκέω
323 ἀσπαίρω
324 ἀτιμάζω
325 ἀτιμάω
326 ἀτιτάλλω
327 ἀτύζομαι
328 ἀφύσσω
329 ἀχεύω

Verbs Occurring 10–25 Times

330 ἄω	363 ἑλελίζω	396 κεάζω
331 βάζω	364 ἑλίσσω	397 κεδάννυμι
332 βασιλεύω	365 ἐμπάζομαι	398 κείω
333 βιάω	366 ἐναίρω	399 κεράννυμι
334 βλάπτω	367 ἐνίπτω	400 κερτομέω
335 βόσκω	368 ἐντύνω	401 κικλήσκω
336 βράχω	369 ἐπαυρίσκω	402 κινέω
337 βρίθω	370 ἐρέσσω	403 κλάζω
338 γέγωνα	371 ἐρητύω	404 κλάω
339 γνάμπτω	372 ἔρρω	405 κλονέω
340 γουνόομαι	373 ἔρυμαι	406 κοιρανέω
341 δαΐζω	374 ἐρωέω	407 κορέω (fut.)
342 δακρύω	375 ἔσθω	408 κοσμέω
343 δάμνημι	376 εὐνάω	409 κοτέω
344 δειπνέω	377 εὐχετάομαι	410 κραιαίνω
345 δέμω	378 ἐχθαίρω	411 κρατέω
346 δέρκομαι	379 ζεύγνυμι	412 κρύπτω
347 δέρω	380 ζώννυμι	413 κυκάω
348 δεύω	381 ἡβάω	414 κυνέω
349 δηλέομαι	382 θαμβέω	415 κωκύω
350 δηόω, δηιόω	383 θάπτω	416 λάζομαι
351 διδάσκω	384 θαρσέω	417 λείβω
352 δίεμαι	385 θαρσύνω	418 λεύσσω
353 δίζημαι	386 θείνω	419 λιάζομαι
354 δινέω	387 θέλγω	420 λιλαίομαι
355 δοάσσατο	388 θηέομαι	421 λοέω
356 ἐγγυαλίζω	389 θύνω	422 λοχάω
357 ἐέλδομαι, ἔλδομαι	390 θύω	423 μαίνομαι
358 ἔθω	391 ἰαίνω	424 μαίομαι
359 εἴβω	392 ἰαύω	425 μαντεύομαι
360 εἰλύω	393 ἰθύω	426 μάρπτω
361 εἰρύομαι	394 καθαίρω	427 μαστίζω
362 ἐΐσκω	395 καίνυμαι	428 μέδομαι

429 μειδάω
430 μέμονα
431 μενοινώω
432 μηνίω
433 μητιάω
434 μηχανάω
435 μιστύλλω
436 μύρομαι
437 νεικείω
438 νήχω
439 νίζω
440 νίπτω
441 νίσομαι, νίσσομαι
442 νοσφίζομαι
443 ξεινίζω
444 οἴγνυμι
445 οἰμώζω
446 διστεύω
447 ὀλέκω
448 ὁμιλέω
449 ὁμοκλάω, -έω
450 ὀμόργνυμι
451 ὀνίνημι
452 ὄνομαι
453 ὀνομαίνω
454 ὀπτάω
455 ὀπυίω
456 ὄσσομαι
457 ὀφέλλω
458 ὀχέω
459 παλάσσω
460 παμφανόω
461 πατέομαι

462 πεδάω
463 πειρητίζω
464 πείρω
465 πελεμίζω
466 πένομαι
467 πετάννυμι
468 πιφαύσκω
469 ποθέω
470 πρέπω
471 πρήθω
472 προβλώσκω
473 πτύσσω
474 πτώσσω
475 πυκάζω
476 πωλέομαι
477 ῥαίω
478 ῥιγέω
479 ῥίπτω
480 ῥύομαι
481 ῥώομαι
482 σείω
483 σημαίνω
484 σκεδάννυμι
485 σκίδναμαι
486 σπάω
487 σπέρχω
488 σπεύδω
489 στείχω
490 στέλλω
491 στεναχίζω
492 στορέννυμι
493 στρωφάω
494 στυγέω

495 στυφελίζω
496 συλάω
497 σφάζω
498 ταρβέω
499 τέθηπα
500 τελέθω
501 τετίημαι
502 τήκω
503 τινάσσω
504 τιταίνω
505 τιτύσκομαι
506 τμήγω
507 τολμάω
508 τρέω
509 τρίβω
510 τρομέω
511 τρύχω
512 τρωπάω
513 ὑφαίνω
514 φαείνω
515 φέβομαι
516 φείδομαι
517 φθέγγομαι
518 φθινύθω
519 φθονέω
520 φοιτάω
521 φυτεύω
522 χαλεπαίνω
523 χανδάνω
524 χραισμέω
525 χράομαι
526 χρίω

NOUNS

LIST VII
NOUNS OCCURRING 500–1,000 TIMES

1 ἀνήρ	3 θυμός	5 υἱός
2 θεός	4 νηῦς	6 χείρ

LIST VIII
NOUNS OCCURRING 200–500 TIMES

7 ἄναξ	15 ἔργον	23 ξεῖνος
8 γαῖα	16 ἕταρος, ἑταῖρος	24 παῖς
9 γέρων	17 ἵππος	25 πατήρ
10 γυνή	18 λαός	26 πόλεμος
11 δόρυ	19 μέγαρον	27 πόλις
12 δῶμα	20 μήτηρ	28 πούς
13 ἔγχος	21 μνηστήρ	29 φρήν
14 ἔπος	22 μῦθος	30 χαλκός

LIST IX
NOUNS OCCURRING 100–200 TIMES

31 αἷμα	43 δόμος	55 κῦμα
32 ἄλοχος	44 δῶρον	56 κύων
33 ἅλς	45 ἥλιος	57 μάχη
34 ἄνεμος	46 ἦμαρ	58 μένος
35 ἄνθρωπος	47 ἥρως	59 μοῖρα
36 ἄστυ	48 ἠώς	60 νόος
37 βασιλεύς	49 θάλασσα	61 νύξ
38 βίη	50 θάνατος	62 οἶκος
39 βοῦς	51 θεά	63 οἶνος
40 γόνυ	52 κεφαλή	64 ὀφθαλμός
41 δάκρυ	53 κλισίη	65 πεδίον
42 δῆμος	54 κούρη	66 πόντος

67 ποταμός
68 πῦρ
69 στῆθος
70 τεῖχος
71 τεῦχος
72 τόξον
73 ὕδωρ
74 ὕπνος
75 χρώς
76 ὦμος

LIST X

Nouns Occurring 50–100 Times

77 ἀγορή
78 αἴξ
79 ἄλγος
80 ἀλκή
81 ἀμφίπολος
82 ἅρμα
83 ἀσπίς
84 ἄχος
85 βέλος
86 βοή
87 βουλή
88 γόος
89 γυῖα (pl.)
90 δαίμων
91 δαίς
92 δέπας
93 δίφρος
94 δμωή
95 εἷμα
96 εὐνή
97 ἦτορ
98 θάλαμος
99 θεράπων
100 θρόνος
101 θύρη
102 κάρη
103 κήρ
104 κῆρ
105 κῆρυξ
106 κλέος
107 κονίη
108 κραδίη
109 κτῆμα
110 κῦδος
111 λέων
112 μῆλον
113 νέκυς
114 νῆσος
115 νόστος
116 ξίφος
117 ὁδός
118 ὄϊς
119 ὀϊστός
120 ὄλεθρος
121 ὅμιλος
122 ὄρος
123 ὄσσε
124 οὐρανός
125 ὄχος
126 πέτρη
127 ποιμήν
128 πόνος
129 πόσις
130 πότνια
131 πύλη
132 σάκος
133 σῆμα
134 σῖτος
135 στρατός
136 συβώτης
137 σῦς
138 τέκνον
139 τέκος
140 φάος
141 φιλότης
142 φώς
143 χθών
144 χιτών
145 χλαίνη
146 χόλος
147 χρή
148 χρυσός
149 ψυχή

LIST XI

Nouns Occurring 25–50 Times

150 ἀγγελίη
151 ἄγγελος
152 ἀγρός
153 ἀγών
154 ἄεθλον
155 ἄεθλος
156 ἀήρ
157 αἶα
158 αἰδώς
159 αἰθήρ
160 αἶσα
161 αἰχμή
162 αἰχμητής
163 ἀνάγκη
164 ἀοιδή
165 ἀοιδός
166 ἄποινα
167 Ἀργειφόντης
168 ἀρετή
169 ἄρης
170 ἀριστεύς
171 ἄρνα
172 ἄρουρα
173 ἀρχός
174 ἄτη
175 αὐλή
176 αὐτή
177 αὐχήν
178 βίοτος
179 βλέφαρον

180 βορέης
181 γάμος
182 γαστήρ
183 γενεή
184 γένος
185 γέρας
186 γῆρας
187 δεῖπνον
188 δέμας
189 δεσμός
190 δηιοτής
191 δμώς
192 δόλος
193 δόρπον
194 ἐδητύς
195 ἔθνος
196 εἶδος
197 ἑκατόμβη
198 ἔλαιον
199 ἐνιαυτός
200 ἔντεα
201 ἐπίκουρος
202 ἐρετμόν
203 ἔρις
204 ἕρκος
205 ἔρος
206 ζυγόν
207 ἡγεμών
208 ἡγήτωρ
209 ἡμίονος

210 ἡνία
211 ἡνίοχος
212 ἤπειρος
213 θέμις
214 θίς
215 θώρηξ
216 ἰός
217 ἱππεύς
218 ἱππότα
219 ἱρόν, ἱερόν
220 ἴς
221 ἱστός
222 κακότης
223 κάματος
224 κασίγνητος
225 κέλευθος
226 κῆδος
227 κληίς
228 κόρυς
229 κορυφή
230 κοῦρος
231 κράτος
232 κρατός (gen.)
233 κρέας
234 κρητήρ
235 κυνέη
236 λέχος
237 λίθος
238 λιμήν
239 μέδων

240 μηρός
241 μῆτις
242 νεῖκος
243 νεφεληγερέτα
244 νέφος
245 νίκη
246 νύμφη
247 νῶτον
248 ὀδούς
249 ὀδύνη
250 οἰωνός
251 ὅρκιον
252 ὅρκος
253 ὄρνις
254 ὄρχαμος
255 ὀστέον
256 οὔατος (gen.)
257 οὖδας
258 οὐδός

259 ὄψ
260 πένθος
261 πῆμα
262 πομπή
263 πόσις
264 πότμος
265 πρόμαχος
266 πτόλεμος
267 πτολίεθρον
268 πτόλις
269 πύργος
270 πυρή
271 ῥόος
272 σθένος
273 σίδηρος
274 σκῆπτρον
275 σπέος
276 σταθμός
277 στίξ

278 στόμα
279 τάφρος
280 τέλος
281 τιμή
282 τοκεύς
283 τράπεζα
284 τρίπος
285 ὕλη
286 ὑσμίνη
287 φάλαγξ
288 φάρμακον
289 φᾶρος
290 φάσγανον
291 φόβος
292 φόνος
293 φωνή
294 χρόνος
295 χῶρος
296 ὥρη

LIST XII
Nouns Occurring 10-25 Times

297 ἀγός
298 ἄγυια
299 ἀδελφεός
300 ἀέθλιον
301 ἄελλα
302 αἰγίς
303 αἰετός
304 αἴθουσα
305 αἰπόλος
306 αἰών
307 ἄκοιτις

308 ἀκτή
309 ἀκωκή
310 ἀλήτης
311 ἀλοιφή
312 ἄλφιτον
313 ἀλωή
314 ἅμαξα
315 ἀμβροσίη
316 ἄνθος
317 ἄντρον
318 ἄντυξ

319 ἄορ
320 ἀπήνη
321 ἄργυρος
322 ἀρή
323 ἀρχή
324 ἀσπιστής
325 ἀστήρ
326 ἀτασθαλίη
327 αὐγή
328 αὐδή
329 ἀυτμή

Nouns Occurring 10-25 Times

330 ἀφραδίη	363 ἐδωδή	396 ἱκέτης
331 ἀχλύς	364 ἐέλδωρ	397 ἴκρια (pl.)
332 βασίλεια	365 εἶδαρ	398 ἱμάς
333 βένθος	366 εἴδωλον	399 ἵμερος
334 βῆσσα	367 ἐλαίη	400 ἰότης
335 βιός	368 ἔλαφος	401 ἱππηλάτα
336 βουκόλος	369 ἐλέφας	402 ἱστίον
337 βωμός	370 ἕλκος	403 ἰχθύς
338 γαμβρός	371 ἔναρα (pl.)	404 κάλλος
339 γῆ	372 ἐπαλξις	405 κάνεον
340 γλῶσσα	373 Ἐρινύς	406 καπνός
341 γόνος	374 ἐρωή	407 κάπρος
342 γρηῦς	375 ἐσθής	408 κάρηνα
343 δαΐς	376 ἐσχάρη	409 καρπός
344 δάπεδον	377 ἐσχατιή	410 καρπός
345 δειρή	378 ἔτος	411 κάρτος
346 δέμνιον	379 εὖχος	412 κασιγνήτη
347 δένδρεον	380 εὐχωλή	413 κασσίτερος
348 δέος	381 ἐφετμή	414 κειμήλιον
349 δέρμα	382 ζέφυρος	415 κέρας
350 δέσποινα	383 ζόφος	416 κεραυνός
351 δημός	384 ζωστήρ	417 κέρδος
352 διάκτωρ	385 ἥβη	418 κίων
353 δίκη	386 ἠιών	419 κλῆρος
354 δοῦπος	387 ἠχή	420 κλισμός
355 δρόμος	388 θάρσος	421 κνέφας
356 δρῦς	389 θαῦμα	422 κνήμη
357 δύναμις	390 θήρ	423 κνίση
358 δῶ	391 θρῆνυς	424 κοῖτος
359 ἐγκέφαλος	392 θρίξ	425 κόλπος
360 ἐγχείη	393 θύελλα	426 κόμη
361 ἔδος	394 ἰαχή	427 κώμυς
362 ἕδρη	395 ἱδρώς	428 κρήδεμνον

429 κρήνη
430 κρόταφος
431 κτέαρ
432 κτῆσις
433 κτύπος
434 κύπελλον
435 κῶας
436 λᾶας
437 λαῖλαψ
438 λέβης
439 λειμών
440 λέκτρον
441 ληίς
442 λίμνη
443 λοιγός
444 λόφος
445 λόχος
446 λώβη
447 μάζος
448 μαῖα
449 μάντις
450 μάστιξ
451 μέγεθος
452 μείς, μήν
453 μελίη
454 μέλος
455 μετάφρενον
456 μέτρον
457 μέτωπον
458 μήδεα (pl.)
459 μῆνις
460 μηρία (pl.)
461 μήστωρ

462 μητίετα
463 μόρος
464 μοῦσα
465 μυχός
466 ναύτης
467 νεβρός
468 νευρή
469 νεφέλη
470 νηός
471 νόημα
472 νομεύς
473 νότος
474 ξείνιον
475 ξύλον
476 ὄβελος
477 ὄζος
478 διζύς
479 οἰκία (pl.)
480 οἶτος
481 ὄλβος
482 ὅμαδος
483 ὄμβρος
484 ὁμηλικίη
485 ὄμμα
486 ὄνειαρ
487 ὄνειδος
488 ὄνειρος
489 ὄνομα, οὔνομα
490 ὅπλον
491 ὀρυμαγδός
492 οὖρος
493 ὀφρύς
494 ὀχεύς

495 ὄχθη
496 παλάμη
497 παράκοιτις
498 παρειά
499 πάτρη
500 πέδιλα (pl.)
501 πεῖραρ
502 πέλεκυς
503 πέπλος
504 πληθύς
505 πνοιή
506 ποθή
507 ποινή
508 πολεμιστής
509 πομπός
510 ποτόν
511 πραπίς
512 πρόθυρον
513 πρόσωπον
514 πρυμνήσιον
515 πτερόν
516 πῶυ
517 ῥάβδος
518 ῥάκος
519 ῥέεθρον
520 ῥηγμίς
521 ῥῆγος
522 ῥινός
523 ῥίς
524 ῥοή
525 σανίς
526 σέλας
527 σίαλος

528 σκόπελος	543 τέρας	558 φῦλον
529 σκοπιή	544 τοῖχος	559 φύλοπις
530 σκοπός	545 τρόμος	560 χαίτη
531 σκότος	546 τροφός	561 χάρις
532 σπουδή	547 τρυφάλεια	562 χάρμη
533 στέρνον	548 τύμβος	563 χεῖλος
534 στοναχή	549 ὕβρις	564 χερμάδιον
535 σχεδίη	550 ὑπερώιον	565 χέρσος
536 τάλαντον	551 ὗς	566 χορός
537 ταμίη	552 ὑφορβός	567 χρειώ
538 τάπης	553 φαρέτρη	568 χρεώ
539 ταῦρος	554 φλόξ	569 χρῆμα
540 τέκτων	555 φόρμιγξ	570 ψάμαθος
541 τελαμών	556 φυή	571 ψεῦδος
542 τέμενος	557 φύλλον	572 ὠτειλή

PRONOUNS, ADJECTIVES, ADVERBS, PREPOSITIONS, ETC.

LIST XIII

PRONOUNS, ADJECTIVES, ADVERBS, PREPOSITIONS, ETC., OCCURRING 500–10,000 TIMES

1 ἀλλά
2 ἄλλος
3 ἄρα
4 αὐτάρ
5 αὐτός
6 γάρ
7 γέ
8 δέ
9 δή
10 ἐγώ
11 εἰ
12 εἰς, ἐς
13 ἐκ, ἐξ
14 ἐν, ἐνί
15 ἔνθα
16 ἐπεί
17 ἐπί
18 ἤ, ἠέ
19 ἦ
20 ἠδέ
21 καί
22 κατά, κάδ
23 κέ
24 μάλα
25 μέγας
26 μέν
27 μή
28 μίν
29 νῦν
30 ὁ, ἡ, τό
31 ὅς, ἥ, ὅ
32 ὅτε
33 οὐ, οὐκ
34 οὗ
35 οὐδέ
36 παρά
37 πᾶς
38 περ
39 πολλός
40 σύ
41 τὶς, τὶ
42 φίλος
43 ὡς
44 ὥς, ὧς

LIST XIV

PRONOUNS, ADJECTIVES, ADVERBS, PREPOSITIONS, ETC., OCCURRING 200–500 TIMES

45 ἀθάνατος
46 ἅμα
47 ἀμφί
48 ἄν
49 ἀνά
50 ἀπό
51 ἄριστος
52 αὖτε
53 διά
54 δῖος
55 ἕκαστος
56 ἐμός
57 ἑός
58 ἔπειτα
59 ἔτι
60 εὖ
61 ἡμεῖς
62 κακός
63 καλός
64 μετά
65 ὅδε
66 ὅσος
67 ὅς τε
68 οὔτε

69 οὗτος
70 ὄφρα
71 περί
72 ποτί

73 πρός, προτί, ποτί
74 σός
75 σύν
76 σφεῖς

77 τότε
78 ὑπό
79 ὤ, ὦ

LIST XV

Pronouns, Adjectives, Adverbs, Prepositions, etc., Occurring 100–200 Times

80 ἀγαθός
81 αἰ
82 αἰεί
83 αἶψα
84 ἀλλήλων
85 ἀμύμων
86 ἀμφοτέρω
87 ἅπας
88 ἀτάρ
89 αὖ
90 αὐτίκα
91 αὖτις
92 ἄψ
93 βροτός
94 δύο, δύω
95 ἐνθάδε
96 ἐσθλός

97 εὐρύς
98 ἤδη
99 θοός
100 ἵνα
101 κεῖνος
102 κρατερός
103 μάλιστα
104 μέγα, μεγάλα
105 μέλας
106 μέσος
107 μηδέ
108 νύ
109 ὅθι
110 οἷος
111 οἶος
112 ὀξύς
113 ὅστις

114 πάρος
115 πατρίς
116 πολύς
117 πολύ
118 ποῦ
119 πρίν
120 πρῶτον, πρῶτα
121 πρῶτος
122 πτερόεις
123 πώ
124 τίς, τί
125 τῶ (τῷ)
126 ὑμεῖς
127 ὧδε
128 ὠκύς

LIST XVI

Pronouns, Adjectives, Adverbs, Prepositions, etc., Occurring 50–100 Times

129 ἀγλαος
130 ἄγχι
131 αἰγίοχος
132 αἰέν

133 αἰνός
134 αἰπύς
135 ἀμείνων
136 ἄμφω

137 ἄντα
138 ἀντίθεος
139 ἀντίον
140 ἀργαλέος

Pronouns, etc., Occurring 25–50 Times

141 αὖθι	166 λυγρός	191 πρό
142 αὐτοῦ	167 μακρός	192 προπάροιθε
143 αὔτως	168 μᾶλλον	193 πρόσθεν
144 γλαυκῶπις	169 μεγάθυμος	194 πρότερος
145 γλαφυρός	170 μεγαλήτωρ	195 πυκινός
146 δαΐφρων	171 νέος	196 πως
147 δεινός	172 νήπιος	197 σχεδόν
148 δεῦρο	173 νῶι	198 τάχα
149 διοτρεφής	174 οἴκαδε	199 ταχύς
150 εἷς	175 ὄπισθε, ὄπιθε	200 τάχιστα
151 ἶσος	176 ὀπίσω	201 τί
152 εἴσω	177 ὁπότε, ὁππότε	202 τοῖος
153 ἔνδον	178 ὅπως, ὅππως	203 τοιοῦτος
154 ἕνεκα, εἵνεκα	179 ὅτι	204 τόσσος
155 ἕτερος	180 ὅτις	205 τόφρα
156 ζωός	181 οὐκέτι	206 ὑπέρ
157 ἠμέν	182 οὖν	207 ὑψηλός
158 ἡμέτερος	183 οὕνεκα	208 φαεινός
159 θεῖος	184 οὕτως	209 φαίδιμος
160 ἱερός, ἱρός	185 πάλιν	210 χαλεπός
161 ἶσος	186 περικαλλής	211 χάλκεος
162 κλυτός	187 περίφρων	212 χρύσειος
163 κοῖλος	188 πολλόν	213 χρύσεος
164 κρείων	189 πολύμητις	214 ὦκα
165 λευκός	190 πόποι	215 ὥς τε

LIST XVII

Pronouns, Adverbs, Adjectives, Prepositions, etc., Occurring 25–50 Times

216 ἀγαυός	220 ἀεικής	224 ἄκρος
217 ἀγήνωρ	221 ἀέκων	225 ἀλεγεινός
218 ἄγριος	222 αἰδοῖος	226 ἅλις
219 ἀγχοῦ	223 αἶθοψ	227 ἄλκιμος

228 ἄλλοτε
229 ἀμβρόσιος
230 ἀμφίς
231 ἀντικρύ
232 ἀντίος
233 ἀολλής
234 ἀπάνευθε
235 ἀργύρεος
236 ἀρήιος
237 ἀρηίφιλος
238 ἄσπετος
239 ἆσσον
240 ἀτάλαντος
241 ἀτρεκέως
242 αὐτόθι
243 ἄφαρ
244 ἀφνειός
245 βαθύς
246 βαρύς
247 γεραιός
248 δειλός
249 δεινόν
250 δεξιός
251 δήιος
252 δήν
253 δηρόν
254 διαμπερές
255 διογενής
256 δοιώ
257 δολιχόσκιος
258 δουρικλυτός, δουρικλειτός
259 δυσμενής

260 δώδεκα
261 ἐγγύθεν
262 ἐγγύς
263 εἴκοσι, ἐείκοσι
264 ἐκεῖνος
265 ἔμπεδος
266 ἔμπης
267 ἔνθεν
268 ἐννοσίγαιος
269 ἐνοσίχθων
270 ἔντοσθε
271 ἐπήν
272 ἑτέρωθεν
273 εὐκνήμις
274 ἐυκτίμενος
275 εὐπλόκαμος
276 ἐύς, ἠύς
277 ἐύσσελμος
278 εὖτε
279 ἕως, εἵως, εἷος
280 ἡδύς
281 ἦμος
282 ἤν
283 ἤπιος
284 ἠριγένεια
285 ἦτε
286 ἠύτε
287 θαλερός
288 θεοειδής
289 θεσπέσιος
290 θνητός
291 θοῦρος
292 θύραζε

293 ἰδέ
294 ἰθύς
295 ἱππόδαμος
296 ἴφθιμος
297 καρπαλίμως
298 καρτερός
299 κερδίων
300 κομόωντε
301 κορυθαίολος
302 κυδάλιμος
303 λευκώλενος
304 λίην
305 μάκαρ
306 μακρόν, μακρά
307 μαλακός
308 μέγιστος
309 μείζων
310 μειλίχιος
311 μετόπισθε
312 μήτε
313 μοῦνος
314 μυρίος
315 μώνυξ
316 νέον
317 νηλεής, νηλής
318 νημερτής
319 νόσφι
320 ξανθός
321 ὄβριμος
322 ὀλίγος
323 ὀλοός
324 ὁμοῖος
325 ὁμῶς

PRONOUNS, ETC., OCCURRING 10-25 TIMES 25

326 ὅσον
327 πάγχυ
328 πάμπαν
329 πάντῃ
330 παντοῖος
331 πάντοσε
332 πάροιθε
333 παχύς
334 πεζός
335 πίων
336 πλέων (πλείων)
337 πλεῖστος
338 ποδώκης
339 ποικίλος
340 πολιός
341 πολύτλας
342 πορφύρεος

343 πρόφρων
344 πρυμνός
345 πυκνός
346 πῶς
347 ῥεῖα, ῥέα
348 ῥοδοδάκτυλος
349 σιωπῇ
350 σμερδαλέον
351 στιβαρός
352 στυγερός
353 σχέτλιος
354 τεός
355 τῇ
356 τῆλε
357 τίπτε
358 τοιόσδε
359 τόσσον

360 τούνεκα
361 τρεῖς
362 τρίς
363 ὕπερθε
364 ὑπέρθυμος
365 ὑπερφίαλος
366 ὑπόδρα
367 φέρτερος
368 φίλτατος
369 χάλκειος
370 χαλκήρης
371 χαλκοχίτων
372 χαμᾶζε
373 ὡσεί
374 ὥς περ

LIST XVIII

PRONOUNS, ADVERBS, ADJECTIVES, PREPOSITIONS, ETC., OCCURRING 10-25 TIMES

375 ἅ
376 ἄαπτος
377 ἀγακλειτός
378 ἀγανός
379 ἀγχίμολος
380 ἀδινός
381 ἀεικέλιος
382 ἀέκητι
383 ἀθρόος
384 αἰειγενέτης
385 αἰζηός
386 αἴθε

387 αἰθόμενος
388 αἴθων
389 αἱματόεις
390 αἰνότατος
391 αἰπεινός
392 αἴσιμος
393 αἴτιος
394 ἀκάματος
395 ἀκαχμένος
396 ἀκέων
397 ἀκήν
398 ἀκρότατος

399 ἄκων
400 ἅλιος
401 ἄλιος
402 ἄλλῃ
403 ἀλλοδαπός
404 ἄλλοθεν
405 ἀλλότριος
406 ἄλλυδις
407 ἄλλως
408 ἄμβροτος
409 ἀμήχανος
410 ἄμυδις

411 ἀμφιγυήεις
412 ἀμφιέλισσα
413 ἀμφικύπελλον
414 ἀμφοτέρωθεν
415 ἀναιδής
416 ἄναλκις
417 ἀνδροφόνος
418 ἄνευθε
419 ἄντην
420 ἀντί
421 ἀντία
422 ἄξιος
423 ἀπαλός
424 ἀπείρων
425 ἀπερείσιος
426 ἀπήμων
427 ἀπηνής
428 ἀργιόδους
429 ἀργυρόηλος
430 ἀργυρόπεζα
431 ἀργυρότοξος
432 ἀρείων
433 ἀριστερός
434 ἀρνειός
435 ἄρσην
436 ἀσάμινθος
437 ἄσβεστος
438 ἀσπάσιος
439 ἀσπασίως
440 ἀστερόεις
441 ἀτάσθαλος
442 ἀτειρής
443 ἄτερ
444 ἀτρύγετος

445 αὔριον
446 ἄφρων
447 βόειος
448 βουληφόρος
449 βοῶπις
450 βροτολοιγός
451 γαιήοχος
452 γλυκερός
453 γλυκύς
454 γναμπτός
455 γνωτός
456 γυμνός
457 δαιδάλεος
458 δαιμόνιος
459 δακρυόεις
460 δέκα
461 δέκατος
462 δεξιτερός
463 δεύτερον
464 δεύτερος
465 δηθά
466 διίφιλος
467 δίκαιος
468 δινήεις
469 δίχα
470 δολιχός
471 δυοκαίδεκα
472 δύστηνος
473 ἐγγύθι
474 εἴκελος
475 εἰλίπος
476 ἑκάεργος
477 ἑκάς
478 ἑκάτερθε

479 ἴκηλος
480 ἐκτός
481 ἔκτοσθε
482 ἑκών
483 ἕλιξ
484 ἔμπεδον
485 ἐναίσιμος
486 ἐναλίγκιος
487 ἐναντίβιον
488 ἐναντίον
489 ἐναντίος
490 ἐνδόθι
491 ἐνδυκέως
492 ἐννέα
493 ἐννῆμαρ
494 ἐντός
495 ἕξ
496 ἐξαπίνης
497 ἐξαῦτις
498 ἐξείης
499 ἔξοχον, ἔξοχα
500 ἔξοχος
501 ἐπιείκελος
502 ἐπιεικής
503 ἐπισταμένως
504 ἐπιχθόνιος
505 ἑπτά
506 ἐρατεινός
507 ἐριβῶλαξ
508 ἐρίγδουπος, ἐρί-
    δουπος
509 ἐρίηρος
510 ἐρικυδής
511 ἐρυθρός

512 ἐσσυμένως
513 ἐτεόν
514 ἐτέρωσε
515 ἐτήτυμον
516 ἑτοῖμος
517 εὔδμητος
518 εὐεργής
519 ἐΰξεστος
520 ἐΰξοος
521 εὐρυάγυιος
522 εὐρύοπα
523 εὐρύχορος
524 ἐΰτυκτος
525 ζείδωρος
526 ἠγάθεος
527 ἠεροειδής
528 ἠμαθόεις
529 ἥμισυς
530 ἠνεμόεις
531 ἠΰκομος
532 ἠῶθεν
533 θαρσαλέος
534 θᾶσσον
535 θερμός
536 θέσφατος
537 θῆλυς
538 θήν
539 θοῶς
540 θρασύς
541 θυμαλγής
542 ἴκελος
543 ἱμερόεις
544 ἴος

545 ἰοχέαιρα
546 ἱππόβοτος
547 ἰσόθεος
548 ἴσον, ἴσα
549 ἶφι
550 ἴφιος
551 ἰχθυόεις
552 καθύπερθε
553 κακῶς
554 καλλίθριξ
555 καλλιπάρῃος
556 κάλλιστος
557 καλλίων
558 καλόν
559 καμπύλος
560 κάρτιστος
561 καταθνητός
562 κεδνός
563 κεῖθεν
564 κεῖθι
565 κεῖσε
566 κελαινεφής
567 κελαινός
568 κλειτός
569 κολλητός
570 κορωνίς
571 κουρίδιος
572 κραιπνός
573 κραταιός
574 κρατερῶς
575 κρείσσων
576 κυάνεος
577 κυανόπρῳρος

578 κύδιστος
579 λάθρῃ
580 λαιψηρός
581 λεπτός
582 λευγαλέος
583 λιγύς
584 λιπαρός
585 μάν
586 μείλινος
587 μελιηδής
588 μελίφρων
589 μενεπτόλεμος
590 μενοεικής
591 μέροψ
592 μεσσηγύ(ς)
593 μηκέτι
594 μήν
595 μίνυνθα
596 ναί
597 νείατος
598 νέρθε
599 νεώτερος
600 νόθος
601 νόστιμος
602 ξεινήιος
603 ξεστός
604 ὅθεν
605 διζυρός
606 οἶνοψ
607 οἷον
608 ὄλβιος
609 ὀλίγον
610 ὁμηγερής

611 ὁμοίος
612 ὁμοῦ
613 ὀμφαλόεις
614 ὀξύ
615 ὀξυόεις
616 ὅπῃ
617 ὁππότερος
618 ὀρθός
619 οὐδείς
620 οὐλόμενος
621 οὖλος
622 οὐρανίων
623 οὐρανόθεν
624 ὄχ(α)
625 ὀψέ
626 παιπαλόεις
627 πάλαι
628 παλαιός
629 πανημέριος
630 παννύχιος
631 παρέκ, παρέξ
632 πατρώιος
633 παῦρος
634 πελώριος
635 πεντήκοντα
636 πέπων
637 περικλυτός
638 πετεηνός
639 πῇ, πῆ
640 πῄ, πή
641 πικρός
642 πιστός
643 πλεῖος

644 πλείων
645 πλησίον
646 πλησίος
647 ποδάρκης
648 ποδήνεμος
649 πόθεν
650 ποθέν
651 ποθί
652 ποιητός
653 ποῖος
654 πολλάκις
655 πολυδαίδαλος
656 πολυμήχανος
657 πολύφρων
658 ποντοπόρος
659 ποῦ
660 πουλυβότειρα
661 πρηνής
662 πρόπας
663 πρόσ(σ)ω
664 προτέρω
665 πρώτιστος
666 πτολίπορθος
667 πτωχός
668 πύκα
669 πυκινῶς
670 πύματος
671 ῥηιδίως
672 ῥίμφα
673 σάφα
674 σήμερον
675 σιγαλόεις
676 σιγῇ

677 σιδήρεος
678 σκιόεις
679 σμερδαλέος
680 σόος
681 σῶς
682 στονόεις
683 σφέτερος
684 σφός
685 ταλασίφρων
686 ταχύπωλος
687 τέρην
688 τερπικέραυνος
689 τεσσαράκοντα
690 τέσσαρες
691 τέως, τείως, τεῖος
692 τηλόθεν
693 τηλόθι
694 τηλοῦ
695 τοιγάρ
696 τοῖον
697 τοσόσδε
698 τρηχύς
699 τρίτατος
700 τρίτος
701 τυτθόν, τυτθά
702 τυτθός
703 ὑγρός
704 ὑλήεις
705 ὑμέτερος
706 ὕπατος
707 ὑπένερθε
708 ὑπερηνορέων
709 ὑπερμενής

PRONOUNS, ETC., OCCURRING 10-25 TIMES

710 ὕπτιος
711 ὕστατον, ὕστατα
712 ὕστερον
713 ὑψερεφής
714 ὕψοσε
715 φέρτατος
716 φιλοπτόλεμος
717 χαμάδις
718 χαμαί
719 χαρίεις
720 χείρων
721 χερείων
722 χλωρός
723 χρυσόθρονος
724 ὠκύπορος
725 ὠκύπος

ENGLISH LISTS

VERBS

LIST I
VERBS OCCURRING 500–2,000 TIMES

1. Lead
2. Go
3. Throw, smite
4. Give
5. Am
6. Go
7. Spoke, said
8. Come, go
9. Have
10. Set, stand
11. See
12. Make, put
13. Say, declare

LIST II
VERBS OCCURRING 200–500 TIMES

14. Take, choose
15. Exchange, answer
16. Speak
17. Become, am born
18. Will, wish
19. Move about, am busy; follow
20. Let go, send
21. Come to, reach
22. Lie, am placed
23. Kill
24. Leave
25. Remain, await
26. Know
27. Lose, destroy
28. Arouse
29. Persuade
30. Fall
31. Bear, bring
32. Flee
33. Speak aloud
34. Pour, shed

LIST III
VERBS OCCURRING 100–200 TIMES

35. Harangue, speak
36. Dart
37. Hear
38. Ward off, defend, assist
39. Bid, command
40. Begin, lead
41. Come to know, know
42. Subdue, tame
43. Dread, fear
44. Accept, receive
45. Am able
46. Enter, put on
47. Let, permit
48. Sit down
49. Say, declare
50. Strike, drive
51. Am like, befit
52. Draw, drag off
53. Pray, vow, declare
54. Sit
55. Die, am killed
56. Arrive at, reach
57. Call, summon
58. Cover, hide

59 Urge, command
60 Go, go away
61 Hearken
62 Take
63 Gather, tell
64 Loose, release
65 Fight
66 Am eager, press on
67 Remind, recall
68 Dwell, inhabit
69 Go, return
70 Perceive, think
71 Depart, am gone
72 Think, expect
73 Urge on
74 Suffer
75 Stop
76 Am
77 Send, escort
78 Breathe, am prudent
79 Work, offer
80 Start, drive; rush
81 End, complete
82 Delight
83 Make
84 Bring forth, beget
85 Turn
86 Show, reveal
87 Point out, show
88 Think, intend
89 Rejoice

LIST IV
VERBS OCCURRING 50–100 TIMES

90 Collect
91 Leap
92 Am king, rule
93 Fasten, lay hold of
94 Fit together, fit
95 Grieve
96 Distribute, feast
97 Bind
98 Awake, arouse
99 Eat
100 See, seem
101 Ask, inquire
102 Drag, draw
103 Make hope, hope
104 Clothe
105 Do, sacrifice
106 Hold back, restrain
107 Sleep
108 Find
109 Live
110 Say, speak
111 Run
112 Sit, cause to sit
113 Hold, check
114 Burn, kindle
115 Command, exhort
116 Find, light upon
117 Weep
118 Lean, sink
119 Separate, decide, select
120 Escape notice; forget (mid.)
121 Pray, entreat
122 Fight
123 Fight
124 Am going, am about
125 Concern, interest
126 Remain, await
127 Mix, mingle
128 Relate, tell
129 Distribute, pasture
130 Return
131 Lament
132 Name
133 Attend, bestow
134 Set in motion; rush
135 Spring
136 Try
137 Sack, waste

Verbs Occurring 25-50 Times

138 Fly
139 Fill
140 Drink
141 Strike, smite
142 Make
143 War
144 Bring to pass; give, grant
145 Learn, ascertain
146 Flow
147 Break
148 Save
149 Turn, twist
150 Cut
151 Stretch
152 Enjoin, charge
153 Value, honor
154 Endure
155 Nourish, rear
156 Kill, slay
157 Waste away, perish
158 Love
159 Bear, carry
160 Enrage, anger
161 Thrust, drive

LIST V
Verbs Occurring 25-50 Times

162 Report, announce
163 Break
164 Hold assembly, speak
165 Sing
166 Respect, scruple
167 Praise
168 Distress, grieve
169 Hurl the javelin, hurl
170 Wander, rove
171 Shun, avoid
172 Ward off, defend, assist
173 Shun, avoid
174 Shun, avoid
175 Miss, err
176 Please
177 Rob, deprive
178 Threaten, menace
179 Disobey
180 Take away
181 Pray, wish, curse
182 Carry off, win
183 Seize, snatch
184 Call aloud
185 Shout
186 Deliberate, advise
187 Will, wish
188 Marry
189 Am born, bear, beget
190 Laugh
191 Rejoice, am glad
192 Wail
193 Teach, learn
194 Kindle, blaze
195 Divide
196 Show, point out
197 Lack
198 Pursue, speed
199 Think, seem
200 Thunder
201 Enter, put on, set
202 Shut off, shut in
203 Yield
204 Crowd together, hem in
205 Drive, strike
206 Pity
207 Pity
208 Despoil, slay
209 Relate
210 Press hard, impel
211 Know how, understand
212 Ask
213 Lean, press down
214 Overthrow, fall down
215 Ask

216 Contend, strive
217 Eat
218 Am leader, command
219 Guide, lead
220 Wonder, admire
221 Leap, spring up
222 Arm with cuirass
223 Send
224 Cry, shriek
225 Sacrifice, slaughter
226 Make straight, direct
227 Reach
228 Work, grow weary
229 Shear, cut down
230 Hide, cover
231 Distress; care for
232 Put to rest, lull
233 Wait upon, convey
234 Knock, smite
235 Arm with helmet, arm
236 Roll
237 Obtain by lot, receive
238 Shine
239 Cease, abate
240 Escape notice
241 Bathe, wash
242 Eagerly desire, am angered, strive
243 Ponder
244 Search after, question
245 Take counsel, devise
246 Woo
247 Toil, suffer
248 Am situated, inhabit
249 Strive, quarrel, upbraid
250 Am angry, take it ill
251 Nod
252 Conquer
253 Prick, pierce
254 Deal out, wield
255 Bewail
256 Take oath
257 Equip, prepare
258 Reach, extend
259 Rouse, move
260 Debate, ponder
261 Stab, wound
262 Stab, wound
263 Owe, ought
264 Am moved, vexed
265 Peer about
266 Bring near
267 Pass through, traverse
268 Fix, build
269 Strike, drive back; wander
270 Sail
271 Labor, am busy
272 Pass over, accomplish
273 Pour, make a libation
274 Groan, lament
275 Stretch
276 Wear out, weary
277 End, complete
278 Prize, honor
279 Atone for, pay
280 Run
281 Hit, happen
282 Strike, hit
283 Am before, anticipate
284 Put to flight
285 Watch, guard
286 Make grow, grow
287 Give way, give over, deprive
288 Show favor, gratify
289 Am troubled, angered
290 Give place, withdraw

LIST VI
VERBS OCCURRING 10–25 TIMES

291 Delude, beguile
292 Admire, am indignant
293 Make to grow, increase
294 Blow
295 Feel shame, reverence
296 Disgrace, insult
297 Ask, demand
298 Beg, importune
299 Hear, perceive
300 Heal
301 Empty, sack
302 Care, am concerned for
303 Anoint
304 Am taken, captured
305 Mow, reap
306 Deny, refuse
307 Meet, encounter
308 Encounter, take part in
309 Encounter, take part in
310 Encounter, take part in
311 Meet, encounter
312 Accomplish
313 Deceive
314 Clatter
315 Pound, shatter
316 Make amends
317 Aid, support
318 Am the best, bravest
319 Protect, help
320 Deny, decline
321 Put in order, arrange
322 Work out
323 Quiver
324 Dishonor, maltreat
325 Dishonor, maltreat
326 Rear, cherish
327 Am dazed, bewildered
328 Draw, dip
329 Grieve
330 Satiate
331 Talk, speak
332 Am king
333 Force, constrain
334 Impede, arrest, harm
335 Feed, pasture
336 Rattle, creak, roar
337 Am heavy, charge
338 Make myself heard, cry out
339 Bend
340 Supplicate, implore
341 Cleave, slay
342 Shed tears, weep
343 Tame, subdue
344 Take a meal
345 Build, construct
346 Look, see
347 Flay
348 Wet, moisten
349 Harm, slay, waste
350 Slay, destroy
351 Teach
352 Am scared away, flee
353 Go to seek, seek to win
354 Whirl
355 Seem, appear
356 Hand over, confer
357 Desire, long for
358 Am wont
359 Shed, let fall
360 Wrap, envelop

361 Drag, rescue
362 Make like, compare to
363 Set quaking, whirl round
364 Curl, wind
365 Care for
366 Slay
367 Chide
368 Make ready, adorn
369 Acquire, enjoy
370 Row
371 Restrain, control
372 Go (painfully)
373 Shield, protect
374 Flow, recede
375 Eat
376 Place in ambush, lay to rest
377 Pray, boast
378 Hate
379 Yoke
380 Gird
381 Am at my youthful prime
382 Wonder at
383 Bury
384 Am bold
385 Encourage
386 Strike
387 Enchant
388 Gaze at, behold
389 Rush on, charge
390 Offer (as burnt offering)
391 Warm, cheer; delight in
392 Sleep, lodge
393 Advance, attack
394 Cleanse
395 Excel
396 Split, cleave
397 Scatter
398 Wish to sleep
399 Mix
400 Taunt, tease
401 Call, summon
402 Move, stir
403 Scream, ring
404 Break
405 Put to rout
406 Am lord, rule
407 Sate, satisfy
408 Arrange, marshal
409 Am angry with
410 Accomplish, fulfil
411 Am superior, rule over
412 Hide, conceal
413 Stir up, mix up
414 Kiss
415 Wail
416 Take
417 Pour, shed
418 See, behold
419 Turn aside, withdraw
420 Desire
421 Bathe, wash
422 Lie in ambush
423 Am mad, rage
424 Seek for, explore
425 Divine, prophesy
426 Seize, overtake
427 Lash, whip
428 Bethink myself of, devise
429 Smile
430 Have in mind, am prompted
431 Ponder, intend
432 Am wroth
433 Deliberate, devise
434 Contrive, perpetrate
435 Cut in small pieces
436 Flow, weep
437 Quarrel, upbraid
438 Swim
439 Wash, wash off
440 Wash, wash off

Verbs Occurring 10–25 Times

441 Go, come, return
442 Depart from, hold aloof
443 Receive, entertain
444 Open
445 Cry out, lament
446 Shoot an arrow
447 Lose, destroy
448 Throng about, go with
449 Shout together, command
450 Wipe away
451 Help
452 Scorn
453 Name, mention
454 Roast
455 Wed, take to wife
456 See, threaten
457 Increase
458 Bear, endure
459 Sprinkle, defile
460 Shine, gleam
461 Taste, enjoy
462 Fetter, constrain
463 Test.
464 Pierce, transfix
465 Shake, brandish
466 Labor over, prepare
467 Spread out
468 Make manifest, make to shine
469 Miss, yearn for
470 Am conspicuous
471 Blow, stream, burn
472 Come forth, go forth
473 Fold
474 Cower, hide
475 Cover closely, wrap up
476 Frequent, consort with
477 Shatter, dash
478 Shudder
479 Fling, hurl
480 Rescue, save
481 Move quickly
482 Shake, brandish
483 Command, point out
484 Scatter, disperse
485 Scatter, disperse
486 Pull, draw
487 Speed, drive fast
488 Am quick, hasten
489 March, move
490 Make ready, send off
491 Sigh, groan
492 Spread, lay
493 Turn constantly, dwell
494 Loathe, hate
495 Smite, knock about
496 Despoil
497 Slaughter
498 Am afraid, dread
499 Am amazed at
500 Am become, be
501 Am troubled
502 Melt
503 Shake, brandish
504 Stretch, draw
505 Aim, prepare
506 Cut, separate
507 Endure, dare
508 Flee, fear
509 Rub, wear out
510 Tremble, quake, dread
511 Exhaust, consume
512 Turn, change
513 Weave
514 Shine
515 Flee, flee from
516 Spare
517 Utter a sound, speak out

518 Waste away, pine
519 Grudge, deny
520 Go to and fro, roam
521 Plant, plan
522 Rage, am angry
523 Hold, contain
524 Help, ward off
525 Have use of, need of
526 Anoint

NOUNS

LIST VII
Nouns Occurring 500–1000 Times

1 Man
2 God
3 Heart, soul, life
4 Ship
5 Son
6 Hand

LIST VIII
Nouns Occurring 200–500 Times

7 Lord, king
8 Earth, land
9 Old man
10 Woman
11 Beam, tree, spear
12 House, room
13 Spear, lance
14 Word
15 Work, deed, thing
16 Companion
17 Horse
18 People, host
19 Hall, dining-hall
20 Mother
21 Suitor
22 Word, saying
23 Stranger, guest, host
24 Child
25 Father
26 War, battle
27 City
28 Foot
29 Diaphragm, mind
30 Copper, bronze

LIST IX
Nouns Occurring 100–200 Times

31 Blood
32 Wife
33 Salt (m.), sea (f.)
34 Wind
35 Man
36 City
37 King
38 Force, violence
39 Cow, ox
40 Knee
41 Tear
42 People
43 House, home
44 Gift
45 Sun
46 Day
47 Hero, warrior
48 Dawn, morning
49 Sea
50 Death
51 Goddess
52 Head
53 Hut
54 Young girl, daughter
55 Wave
56 Dog
57 Fight
58 Might
59 Part, fate
60 Mind, thought
61 Night
62 House

63 Wine
64 Eye
65 Plain
66 Sea, deep
67 River
68 Fire
69 Breast
70 Wall
71 Arms, armor, tackle
72 Bow
73 Water
74 Sleep
75 Skin, body
76 Shoulder

LIST X
Nouns Occurring 50–100 Times

77 Assembly, speech
78 Goat
79 Pain
80 Defense, valor
81 Handmaid
82 Chariot
83 Shield
84 Anguish
85 Missile
86 Shout
87 Counsel, plan
88 Lamentation
89 Joints, limbs
90 Divinity
91 Feast
92 Goblet
93 Chariot, stool
94 Female slave
95 Garment
96 Bed, anchor
97 Heart
98 Chamber
99 Comrade-at-arms
100 Arm chair
101 Door, gate
102 Head
103 Death, fate
104 Heart
105 Herald
106 Rumor, glory
107 Dust, ashes
108 Heart
109 Possession, property
110 Glory, majesty
111 Lion
112 Sheep, goat
113 Corpse
114 Island
115 Return
116 Sword
117 Way, journey
118 Sheep
119 Arrow
120 Destruction
121 Throng
122 Mountain
123 Eyes
124 Heaven
125 Car, chariot
126 Rock, cliff
127 Shepherd
128 Labor, toil
129 Husband, spouse
130 Mistress, queen
131 Gate
132 Shield
133 Sign, token
134 Wheat, food
135 Host, army
136 Swineherd
137 Swine
138 Child
139 Child
140 Light
141 Love, friendship
142 Man
143 Earth, ground
144 Tunic
145 Cloak, mantle
146 Gall, wrath
147 Need
148 Gold
149 Life, soul

LIST XI
Nouns Occurring 25-50 Times

150 Tidings
151 Messenger
152 Field, country
153 Assemblage, game, arena
154 Prize
155 Contest
156 Air
157 Earth, land
158 Shame, respect
159 Sky, upper air
160 Lot, destiny
161 Point, spear
162 Spearman, warrior
163 Necessity, constraint
164 Song
165 Bard
166 Ransom
167 Argeiphontes
168 Excellence
169 Battle, combat
170 Chief
171 Lamb, sheep
172 Plough-land, ground
173 Leader
174 Ruin, folly
175 Courtyard
176 Cry, call
177 Neck
178 Life, substance
179 Eyelid
180 North-wind
181 Marriage
182 Belly, womb
183 Birth, race
184 Family, race
185 Gift of honor, honor
186 Old age
187 Meal, repast
188 Frame, build
189 Fetter, fastening
190 Conflict
191 Slave
192 Deceit
193 Supper
194 Food
195 Host, swarm, herd
196 Appearance
197 Hecatomb
198 Olive-oil
199 Year
200 Armor, weapons
201 Helper in battle
202 Oar
203 Strife
204 Hedge, wall, court
205 Love
206 Yoke, cross-bar
207 Guide, leader
208 Leader, chief
209 Mule
210 Reins
211 Charioteer
212 Land, mainland
213 Law, right
214 Heap, strand
215 Breast-plate, cuirass
216 Arrow
217 Chariot-man
218 Horseman, knight
219 Sacrifice, victim
220 Sinew, strength
221 Mast, loom
222 Evil, cowardice
223 Fatigue, toil
224 Brother
225 Path
226 Care, mourning
227 Bolt, collar-bone, thole-pin
228 Helmet

229 Crest
230 Youth
231 Strength, mastery
232 Head (gen.)
233 Flesh, meat
234 Mixing-bowl
235 Cap, helmet
236 Couch, bed
237 Stone
238 Harbor
239 Ruler, counsellor
240 Thigh
241 Counsel, plan
242 Quarrel
243 Cloud-gatherer
244 Cloud
245 Victory
246 Bride, lady
247 Back
248 Tooth
249 Pain
250 Bird of prey
251 Oath, victim
252 Witness, oath
253 Bird
254 Leader
255 Bone
256 Ear (gen.)
257 Earth, floor
258 Threshold
259 Voice
260 Mourning, grief
261 Woe, harm
262 Dismissal, escort
263 Drink
264 Fate, death
265 Champion
266 War, battle
267 Town, citadel
268 City
269 Tower
270 Pyre
271 Stream
272 Strength
273 Iron
274 Staff, scepter
275 Cave
276 Pen, fold, post
277 Row, rank
278 Mouth
279 Ditch
280 End, completion
281 Price, penalty, honor
282 Parent, ancestor
283 Table
284 Tripod
285 Wood, forest
286 Conflict
287 Line of battle
288 Herb, drug
289 Cloak
290 Sword
291 Flight
292 Murder
293 Voice
294 Time
295 Space, place
296 Season, time

LIST XII

Nouns Occurring 10–25 Times

297 Leader
298 Road, way
299 Brother
300 Prize
301 Gust
302 Aegis
303 Eagle
304 Portico, corridor
305 Goat-herd
306 Life-time, life
307 Wife
308 Shore
309 Point
310 Vagabond
311 Ointment

NOUNS OCCURRING 10–25 TIMES

312 Barley
313 Threshing-floor, vineyard
314 Wagon
315 Ambrosia
316 Blossom, flower
317 Cave
318 Rim
319 Sword
320 Wagon
321 Silver
322 Prayer, curse
323 Beginning
324 Warrior
325 Star
326 Folly
327 Gleam, glow
328 Voice
329 Breath, blast
330 Ignorance, folly
331 Mist, darkness
332 Queen
333 Depth
334 Glen, ravine
335 Bow
336 Herdsman
337 Step, platform, altar
338 Son-in-law, brother-in-law
339 Earth, land
340 Tongue, language
341 Birth, offspring
342 Old woman
343 Torch
344 Ground, pavement
345 Neck, throat
346 Bedstead, bed
347 Tree
348 Fear
349 Skin, hide
350 Mistress
351 Fat
352 Runner, guide
353 Usage, justice
354 Din, thunder
355 Race, racecourse
356 Tree, oak
357 Power, strength
358 House, room
359 Brain
360 Lance
361 Seat, abode
362 Seat
363 Food
364 Desire, wish
365 Food
366 Shape, phantom
367 Olive-tree
368 Stag
369 Ivory
370 Wound, sore
371 Spoils
372 Battlement
373 Erinys
374 Rush, sweep
375 Clothing
376 Hearth
377 Border, edge
378 Year
379 Glory
380 Prayer, boast
381 Command
382 West-wind
383 Darkness, evening
384 Girdle
385 Youth
386 Shore
387 Noise, roar
388 Courage, boldness
389 Wonder
390 Wild beast
391 Foot-stool
392 Hair
393 Blast, gust
394 Cry, shriek
395 Sweat
396 Suppliant
397 Deck, ribs
398 Strap, thong
399 Longing
400 Will
401 Chariot-fighter, knight

402 Sail
403 Fish
404 Beauty
405 Basket
406 Smoke
407 Boar
408 Heads, summits
409 Fruit, grain
410 Wrist
411 Might, mastery
412 Sister
413 Tin
414 Treasure, heirloom
415 Horn
416 Thunder-bolt, lightning
417 Gain, shrewdness
418 Pillar
419 Lot, estate
420 Easy-chair
421 Darkness, dusk
422 Skin
423 Savor, fat
424 Sleep, resting-place
425 Bosom, fold
426 Hair
427 Order, ornament
428 Head-band
429 Spring, fountain
430 Temple (human)
431 Possession, property
432 Property
433 Crash, thunder
434 Cup
435 Fleece
436 Stone
437 Tempest
438 Caldron, basin
439 Meadow
440 Bed
441 Booty
442 Lake
443 Destruction, ruin
444 Crest
445 Ambush
446 Insult
447 Breast
448 Good mother
449 Seer
450 Whip
451 Stature
452 Month
453 Ash-tree, shaft, lance
454 Limb, member
455 Back
456 Measure
457 Forehead, front
458 Plans, counsels
459 Wrath
460 Thigh-pieces
461 Counsellor
462 Counsellor
463 Lot, fate
464 Muse
465 Innermost part, corner
466 Sailor
467 Fawn
468 Sinew, bow-string
469 Cloud
470 Temple
471 Thought, plan
472 Shepherd
473 South-wind
474 Friendly gift
475 Wood, trunk
476 Spit
477 Shoot, twig
478 Woe
479 Abode
480 Fate
481 Fortune, happiness
482 Din
483 Rain
484 Equal age, companion
485 Eye
486 Help, refreshment

Nouns Occurring 10–25 Times

487 Reproach
488 Dream
489 Name
490 Rope, implement, arms
491 Din
492 Fair wind
493 Brow
494 Holder
495 Bank
496 Palm, hand
497 Wife
498 Cheek
499 Native land
500 Sandals
501 End, cord
502 Axe
503 Robe
504 Multitude
505 Breath, blast
506 Yearning, lack
507 Penalty, price
508 Warrior
509 Escort
510 Drink
511 Diaphragm, heart
512 Doorway, porch
513 Face
514 Stern-cable
515 Feather, wing
516 Flock
517 Rod, wand
518 Ragged garment
519 Stream, current
520 Surf
521 Rug, blanket
522 Skin, shield
523 Nose, nostril
524 Flood, stream
525 Board, plank, door
526 Gleam
527 Fat hog
528 Cliff
529 Lookout, watch
530 Watchman
531 Darkness
532 Effort, eagerness
533 Breast, chest
534 Groaning
535 Raft, boat
536 Scale, balance, talent
537 Housekeeper, stewardess
538 Rug, coverlet
539 Bull
540 Builder, carpenter
541 Strap, belt
542 Estate, precinct
543 Prodigy
544 Wall, side
545 Trembling, terror
546 Nurse
547 Helmet
548 Mound, tomb
549 Insolence, violence
550 Upper chamber
551 Swine
552 Swineherd
553 Quiver
554 Flame, blaze
555 Lute, lyre
556 Form
557 Leaf
558 Race, host
559 Combat
560 Hair, mane
561 Grace, charm
562 Joy of battle
563 Lip, rim
564 Stone
565 Land, shore
566 Dancing place, dance
567 Want, need
568 Want, need
569 Possession, property
570 Sand
571 Falsehood
572 Wound

PRONOUNS, ADJECTIVES, ADVERBS, PREPOSITIONS, ETC.

LIST XIII

PRONOUNS, ADJECTIVES, ADVERBS, PREPOSITIONS, ETC., OCCURRING 500–10,000 TIMES

1 But
2 Other, another
3 So then
4 But, however
5 Same, self
6 For, namely
7 At least
8 But, and
9 Now indeed, really
10 I
11 If
12 Into
13 Out, out of
14 In
15 There, where
16 When, since
17 Upon, on
18 Or, than, whether
19 In truth; pray? (affirmative or interrogative)
20 And
21 And, also
22 Down
23 (Anticipatory or potential particle)
24 Very, quite
25 Great, large
26 Indeed
27 Not, lest
28 Him, her, it
29 Now
30 This, he, the, who
31 He, this who
32 When, since
33 Not
34 Him, her
35 Nor, not even
36 Beside, by
37 Every, all
38 Very, at least
39 Much, many
40 Thou
41 Someone, anyone
42 Dear, own
43 As, how, when, that
44 Thus, so

LIST XIV

PRONOUNS, ADJECTIVES, ADVERBS, PREPOSITIONS, ETC., OCCURRING 200–500 TIMES

45 Deathless, immortal
46 At the same time
47 On both sides, about
48 (Anticipatory or potential particle)
49 Up
50 From
51 Best
52 Again, but
53 Through
54 Divine, glorious
55 Each

54 HOMERIC VOCABULARIES

56 My, mine
57 His, her, own
58 Thereupon, then
59 Still, yet
60 Well
61 We
62 Bad, cowardly
63 Beautiful, fine
64 Among, after
65 This
66 How great, how many
67 Who
68 Neither, nor
69 This, that
70 While, until
71 Around, about
72 Ever, once
73 Thereto, to, toward
74 Thy, thine
75 Along with, with
76 Themselves
77 Then, at that time
78 Under
79 O, oh!

LIST XV

PRONOUNS, ADJECTIVES, ADVERBS, PREPOSITIONS, ETC., OCCURRING 100–200 TIMES

80 Good
81 If, whether
82 Always, ever
83 Forthwith
84 One another, each other
85 Blameless
86 Both
87 All
88 But
89 Again, on the other hand
90 Straightway
91 Again, back again
92 Back
93 Mortal
94 Two
95 Hither, here
96 Good
97 Broad
98 Already, now
99 Swift
100 Where, in order that
101 That, that one, he
102 Mighty
103 Most, especially
104 Greatly
105 Dark, black
106 Middle, the middle of
107 But not, nor, not even
108 Now
109 Where
110 Alone
111 Of what sort
112 Sharp
113 Whoever
114 Before, formerly
115 Native
116 Much, many
117 Much, very
118 Anywhere, somewhere
119 Before
120 First
121 First
122 Winged
123 Yet
124 Who?
125 Then, therefore
126 You
127 So, thus
128 Swift

LIST XVI

PRONOUNS, ADJECTIVES, ADVERBS, PREPOSITIONS, ETC., OCCURRING 50–100 TIMES

129 Splendid
130 Near
131 Aegis-holding
132 Always, ever
133 Dreadful
134 Steep, towering
135 Better
136 Both
137 Opposite
138 Godlike
139 Opposite, against
140 Hard, difficult
141 There, here
142 There
143 Merely, as it is
144 Gleaming-eyed
145 Hollow
146 Fiery-hearted
147 Dreadful
148 Hither
149 Zeus-nurtured
150 One
151 Equal, like
152 Within, into
153 Within
154 On account of, for
155 Other, the other
156 Alive
157 Both
158 Our, ours
159 Sacred, godlike
160 Strong, sacred
161 Equal, like
162 Glorious, fine
163 Hollow
164 Ruling
165 Clear, white
166 Miserable
167 Long, tall
168 More
169 Great-hearted
170 Great-hearted, proud
171 New, young
172 Infant
173 We two, both of us
174 Homeward
175 Behind [hind
176 Backward, be-
177 Whenever, when
178 How, that
179 That, because
180 Whoever
181 No longer
182 Therefore, then
183 Wherefore, because
184 Thus
185 Backwards, back
186 Very beautiful
187 Very prudent
188 Much
189 Crafty
190 Alas!
191 Before, forward
192 Before, formerly
193 In front, before
194 Former
195 Close, thick
196 Somehow
197 Near, hard by
198 Quickly, soon
199 Swift
200 Most speedily
201 Somewhat
202 Such, of such a kind
203 Of such a kind, such
204 So great, so much
205 So long
206 Over, in behalf of
207 Lofty
208 Bright

209 Shining, illustrious
210 Hard, difficult
211 Brazen
212 Golden
213 Golden
214 Quickly
215 As, just as

LIST XVII

PRONOUNS, ADVERBS, ADJECTIVES, PREPOSITIONS, ETC., OCCURRING 25–50 TIMES

216 Wondrous, illustrious
217 Valorous
218 Wild, savage
219 Near, hard by
220 Unseemly, disgraceful
221 Unwilling
222 Modest, respected
223 Gleaming
224 Topmost, highest
225 Painful, toilsome
226 Crowded together
227 Valiant
228 At another time
229 Ambrosial, divine
230 On both sides
231 Opposite, straight through
232 Opposite
233 In throngs, together
234 Away, apart from
235 Of silver
236 Warlike
237 Dear to Ares
238 Inexpressible, immense
239 Nearer
240 Like, equal
241 Unerringly, truly
242 There, here
243 Instantly
244 Wealthy, rich in
245 Deep
246 Heavy
247 Old, aged
248 Cowardly, miserable
249 Dreadfully
250 Right (hand), propitious
251 Blazing, hostile
252 Long, for a long time
253 Long, for a long time
254 Through and through, forever
255 Sprung from Zeus
256 Two
257 Long-shadowy
258 Renowned in the use of the spear
259 Hostile
260 Twelve
261 From near, near
262 Near
263 Twenty
264 That one, he
265 Firm, unshaken
266 Wholly, nevertheless
267 Thence, then, whence
268 Earth-shaking
269 Earth-shaking
270 Within

271 When, after
272 On the other side
273 Well-greaved
274 Well-built, well-tilled
275 Fair-tressed
276 Good, noble
277 Well-decked
278 When, as
279 As long as, until
280 Sweet
281 When
282 If
283 Mild
284 Early-born
285 Or, than
286 As
287 Swelling, blooming
288 Godlike
289 Divinely uttered, divine
290 Mortal
291 Impetuous
292 Forth, out
293 And
294 Straight
295 Horse-taming
296 Mighty
297 Swiftly
298 Mighty, stern
299 Better
300 Long-haired
301 With glancing helm
302 Glorious, noble
303 White-armed
304 Too, excessively
305 Blessed
306 Far, afar
307 Soft, gentle
308 Greatest
309 Greater
310 Mild, pleasant
311 Behind
312 Neither, nor
313 Alone
314 Countless
315 Single-hoofed
316 Just now, lately
317 Pitiless
318 Unerring
319 Apart, aloof from, except
320 Yellow, blond
321 Heavy, mighty
322 Little
323 Destructive
324 Like, equal
325 Together, alike
326 As much as, as far as
327 Altogether
328 Altogether
329 On all sides
330 Of all sorts
331 In every direction
332 Before
333 Thick
334 On foot
335 Fat, fertile
336 More, greater
337 Most, a great many
338 Fleet-footed
339 Varied
340 Gray, hoary
341 Much-enduring
342 Purple
343 Cheerful, zealous
344 Extreme, at the end of
345 Close, thick
346 How?
347 Easily
348 Rosy-fingered
349 Silently
350 Terribly
351 Compact, strong
352 Hateful
353 Enduring, hard
354 Thy, thine
355 Here, where
356 Far, far away
357 Why pray?
358 Such

359 So much
360 Therefore
361 Three
362 Thrice
363 From above, above
364 High spirited
365 Mighty, arrogant
366 Sternly, darkly
367 Better, braver
368 Dearest
369 Brazen
370 Bronze-shod
371 Bronze-clad
372 To the ground, down
373 As if
374 Just as

LIST XVIII
Pronouns, Adverbs. Adjectives, Prepositions, Etc., Occurring 10–25 Times

375 Ah!
376 Invincible
377 Renowned
378 Gentle
379 Near, coming near
380 Thick
381 Unseemly, disgraceful
382 Against the will of
383 Together, in crowds
384 Immortal
385 Vigorous
386 Would that
387 Burning, blazing
388 Shining
389 Bloody
390 Most dreadful
391 Steep, towering
392 Destined, due
393 Guilty, to blame
394 Untiring
395 Sharpened, pointed
396 Silent, quiet
397 Silently, silent
398 Topmost, uttermost
399 Javelin
400 Of the sea
401 Fruitless, vain
402 Elsewhere, another way
403 Strange, foreign
404 From elsewhere
405 Of another, strange
406 To another place
407 Otherwise
408 Immortal
409 Helpless, impossible
410 Together, at once
411 Strong in both arms [ends
412 Curved at both
413 Double-cupped
414 On both sides
415 Shameless, pitiless
416 Cowardly
417 Man-slaying
418 Away, apart
419 Opposite, in front
420 Against, instead of
421 Opposite, against
422 Of equal weight, worth

423 Tender
424 Boundless
425 Boundless
426 Unharmed
427 Unfeeling, harsh
428 White-toothed
429 Silver-studded
430 Silver-footed
431 With silver bow
432 Better
433 Left, ill-boding
434 Ram
435 Male
436 Bath-tub
437 Inextinguishable
438 Welcome, glad
439 Gladly
440 Starry
441 Wicked, wanton
442 Unwearied
443 Without, apart from
444 Barren
445 To-morrow
446 Thoughtless, foolish
447 Of an ox, of oxen
448 Counselling
449 Ox-eyed
450 Man-destroying
451 Earth-holding
452 Sweet
453 Sweet
454 Bent
455 Known, related
456 Naked, unarmed
457 Skilfully wrought
458 Possessed
459 Weeping
460 Ten
461 Tenth
462 Right (hand)
463 Secondly, again
464 Second, next
465 Long, a long time
466 Dear to Zeus
467 Right, just
468 Eddying
469 In two
470 Long
471 Twelve
472 Unhappy
473 Near
474 Like
475 Close-footed, trailing-footed
476 Far-working
477 Far, far from
478 On both sides
479 Of good cheer, at ease
480 Outside, outside of
481 Outside, outside of
482 Willing, of one's own will
483 Bent, crook-horned
484 Firmly
485 Fateful, favorable, proper
486 Like
487 With hostile front against
488 Opposite, against
489 Opposite, against
490 Within
491 Duly, kindly
492 Nine
493 For nine days
494 Within
495 Six
496 Suddenly
497 Again, anew
498 In order
499 Chiefly, by far
500 Pre-eminent
501 Like
502 Suitable
503 Skilfully [earth
504 Earthly, upon

505 Seven
506 Lovely
507 With large clods, fertile
508 Resounding
509 Trusty
510 Glorious
511 Red
512 Hastily
513 Truly, truth
514 In the other direction
515 Actually, really
516 Ready
517 Well-built
518 Well-made
519 Well-scraped, polished
520 Well-polished
521 Wide-streeted
522 Wide-thundering
523 With broad lawns
524 Well-wrought
525 Grain-giving
526 Sacred
527 Misty, dim
528 Sandy
529 Half
530 Windy
531 Fair-haired
532 In the morning
533 Daring, bold
534 More speedily
535 Warm
536 Divinely decreed, divine
537 Female
538 Doubtless
539 Swiftly
540 Bold, daring
541 Heart-grieving
542 Like, resembling
543 Passionate, fond, lovely
544 One
545 Pouring arrows
546 Horse-breeding
547 Godlike
548 Equally
549 With might
550 Strong, goodly
551 Abounding in fish
552 From above
553 Badly
554 With beautiful mane, fair-fleeced
555 Fair-cheeked
556 Fairest
557 Fairer
558 Finely
559 Bent, curved
560 Mightiest, best
561 Mortal
562 Careful, good
563 Thence, then
564 There
565 Thither
566 Of dark clouds, dark
567 Dark, black
568 Famous
569 Joined, shod
570 Curved
571 Wedded
572 Quick, hasty
573 Mighty
574 Mightily
575 Stronger, better
576 Dark blue, dark
577 Dark-prowed
578 Most glorious
579 Secretly
580 Nimble, swift
581 Peeled, fine, delicate
582 Mournful
583 Clear, loud
584 Shining, rich
585 Verily, indeed
586 Ashen
587 Honey-sweet
588 Honey-minded, sweet
589 Steadfast in battle

590 Grateful, satisfying
591 Mortal
592 In the middle, between
593 No longer, no more
594 Indeed
595 For a little, a little while
596 Yea
597 Newest, last
598 Below, under
599 Newer, under
600 Illegitimate
601 Of return
602 Of friendship
603 Scraped, polished
604 Whence
605 Wretched
606 Wine-colored
607 As, how
608 Happy, blessed
609 A little
610 Assembled, together
611 Like, equal
612 Together
613 Studded, bossed
614 Sharply, piercingly
615 Sharp-pointed
616 Where, as
617 Whichever
618 Upright, erect
619 No one, nothing
620 Destructive, accursed
621 Thick, woolly
622 Heavenly
623 From heaven
624 By far
625 Late
626 Rugged, rough
627 Long ago
628 Ancient, old
629 All day long
630 All night long
631 Along past, close by
632 Paternal, hereditary
633 Little, few
634 Monstrous, huge
635 Fifty
636 Ripe, dear, coward
637 Renowned
638 Winged, fledged
639 Whither? how?
640 Anywhere, in any way
641 Sharp, bitter
642 Trusty, faithful
643 Full
644 More, greater
645 Near, hard by
646 Near, neighboring
647 Swift-footed
648 Wind-swift
649 Whence?
650 From somewhere
651 At some time, somewhere
652 Made, built
653 Of what sort?
654 Often
655 Much wrought, skilful
656 Much contriving, ever ready
657 Very sagacious
658 Sea-traversing
659 Where? Whither?
660 All-nourishing
661 On the face, head foremost
662 All, all together
663 Forward, in the future
664 Forward, further
665 First of all
666 City-sacking
667 Poor, beggar

668 Thickly, carefully
669 Close, fast
670 Last
671 Easily
672 Swiftly
673 Clearly
674 Today
675 Shining
676 Silently
677 Of iron
678 Shady, shadowy
679 Fearful
680 Safe
681 Safe, certain
682 Mournful, grievous
683 Their
684 Their
685 Stout-hearted
686 With swift steeds
687 Tender
688 Delighting in thunder
689 Forty
690 Four [while
691 So long, mean-
692 From far
693 Far away
694 Afar, far from
695 Accordingly
696 So
697 So great, so much
698 Rough, rugged
699 Third
700 Third
701 Little, a little
702 Little, small
703 Moist, wet
704 Wooded
705 Your, yours
706 Highest, supremest
707 Beneath, below
708 Haughty
709 High-spirited
710 Back, on the back
711 Last
712 Later
713 High-roofed
714 Upward, aloft
715 Best, bravest
716 Fond of war
717 To the ground
718 On the ground
719 Pleasing, graceful
720 Worse, inferior
721 Worse, inferior
722 Green, yellow
723 Golden-throned
724 Swift-sailing
725 Swift-footed

Made in the USA
Lexington, KY
21 January 2018